Who is "She"

"God is within her, "She" will not fail"
Psalm 46:5

Follow & Tag Us On Instagram & Facebook:
@SheHasGoalsJournal
#SheHasGoalsJournal

Website:
www.shehasgoalsjournal.com

Email Us:
customerservice@shehasgoalsjournal.com

© 2021 Kelley's Prints

All rights reserved. This journal or any portion thereof may not be reproduced in any manner whatsoever without written permission of the publisher.

Published by: Kelley's Prints
El Paso, Texas 79925

info@kelleysprints.com

The Goal Accountability Program® (GAP) was created to hold women accountable to self-care one goal at a time.

For corporate bookings and inquiries please email us at
nikela@thegoalaccountabilityprogram.com

She Has Goals®

"She Has Goals"® was created to serve as a personal Accountability Partner. To propel you towards being in a better place mentally, emotionally, spiritually, and physically next week, month and year.

Accountability comes in many forms, we at the GAP believe in having a physical Accountability Partner however, without a plan and system your Partner can only encourage you to a certain level.

Before anyone can hold you accountable, you must create something to be held accountable to and understand you are your only road block.

We will no longer make a mental note of our goals, we will write them down; we will take ownership and defy excuses!

God has equipped you with everything you need to walk in your divine purpose.

My prayer for you in this year:

"May He equip you with all you need for doing His will. May He produce in you, through the power of Jesus Christ, every good thing that is pleasing to Him. All glory to Him forever and ever, Amen!"

Hebrews 13:21

With Love,
Nikela (Nikki) Kelley
"Your Accountability Coach"

How To Use The **She Has Goals**® *Journal* For Optimal Success

Your 2022 Goals

- A big part of goal accomplishment comes from having mental clarity and the ability to organize your thoughts. You can do this by separating your goals into categories.

Your Word/Phrase of The Year

- Based on the goals you've written, choose a word or phrase to describe the year you desire to have.

- This one word/phrase will serve as a personal reminder any time you feel you're getting off track.

- Know and understand the definition of this word/phrase and make sure it speaks to the year you desire to have.

Only choose one word/phrase for optimum focus

Your "Why" Statement

- Your "why" statement should answer why your goals are important to you.

- Your "why" statement should be personal to you and your life. It should explain your motivation and drive. It should push you to keep going every time you read it.

Monthly Pages

- Your goals for the month should be a direct reflection of your goals for the year.

- Write everything that must be done in order to accomplish your goals for the month.

- To create better habits, choose to remain consistent with two things throughout the month.

Weekly Pages

- Work towards your goals by breaking them down into weekly pieces.

- Your weekly sub-tasks are the steps you must take in order to reach your weekly goals.

- Repeat this process each week until you have accomplished your goals for the month.

- Use the last week of the month to complete any lingering tasks/goals you may have.

- Check a box for each day you remained consistent with the habits you chose to create that month.

- Water is a key essential to your health. Track how much water you're drinking daily by coloring a cup each time you complete the 8x8 rule (eight, eight ounce glasses per day).

Daily Focus

- Try to refrain from creating an extensive to-do lists each day. Instead, decide on your top three daily priorities in order to reach your weekly goals.

Moment of Gratitude

- Each week take some time to reflect and write down your weekly wins and or moments of thankfulness.

- Writing the things you are thankful for will help you to continue moving forward anytime you feel down or un-motivated.

Notes Pages

- These pages are for you to jot down any ideas or random thoughts you may have.

Monthly Recap

- This is a time to self reflect and assess your dedication and commitment to your goals.

- Conducting a Monthly Recap allows you to celebrate your accomplishments for the month and analyze the areas you can improve or sustain to reach your goals at a higher rate in the month to come.

- Take this opportunity to reassess the goals you've created for the year along with your "why" statement before moving into the next month. This will keep you focused on your ultimate goals.

- Do not take bad habits into a new month. Correct the mistakes you made in the current month before moving to a new month.

Things To Note

1. Do not to feel obligated to fill each line with goals.
2. Your goals should be intentional and desirable to you, whether big or small.
3. Your goals are your personal aspirations, refrain from measuring your goals to others.
4. Try to refrain from carrying over the same goals day to day, week to week. Start and finish your goals before adding more tasks to your list.
5. Use Sundays to plan your week.
6. When creating your goals make sure they are Specific, Actionable and Time-Associated.

Specific – Precise and clearly defined. These goals should answer who, what, when, where and why.

Actionable – The ability to complete when specific measures are applied.

Time Associated – Create a "no-later-than" date to complete each goal.

2021 Reflection

My 2022 Goals

My *Spiritual* Goals Are:

_____
_____
_____
_____
_____
_____
_____
_____
_____
_____

My *Physical/Health* Goals (To Include Mental & Emotional Are):

_____
_____
_____
_____
_____
_____
_____
_____
_____
_____

My *Family/Relationship* Goals Are:

_____

_____

_____

_____

_____

_____

_____

_____

_____

_____

My *Financial* Goals Are:
Formula: I will save/invest $_____ every pay period for a total of $_____ a month to reach my goal of $_____ a year.

_____

_____

_____

_____

_____

_____

_____

_____

My 2022 Goals

My *Personal* Goals (Career/Business/Education etc.) Are:

My Word/Phrase Of The Year Is:

Only Choose one word/phrase for optimum focus

My "Why" Statement

These Goals Are Important To Me Because:

Month: _____

My Goals This Month, In Alignment With My Yearly Goals Are:

1. Spiritual: _____
2. Physical/Health: _____
3. Family/Relationship: _____
4. Financial: _____
5. Personal: _____

I Will Accomplish These Goals By Doing The Following Things This Month:

_____
_____
_____
_____
_____
_____
_____
_____
_____
_____
_____

I Want To Remain Consistent With The Following Things This Month:

1. _____
2. _____

Tag Us On Instagram: @SheHasGoalsJournal

The Week Of:

In Alignment With My Monthly Goals, This Week I Will Focus On:

1. Spiritual: _____
2. Physical/Health: _____
3. Family/Relationship: _____
4. Financial: _____
5. Personal: _____

Sub-Tasks:

_____
_____
_____
_____

My Consistency Tracker:

| _____ | Mon | Tue | Wed | Thu | Fri | Sat | Sun |
| _____ | Mon | Tue | Wed | Thu | Fri | Sat | Sun |

My Water Consumption This Week (8x8oz Glasses Per-Day)

Monday	☐ ☐ ☐ ☐ ☐ ☐ ☐ ☐
Tuesday	☐ ☐ ☐ ☐ ☐ ☐ ☐ ☐
Wednesday	☐ ☐ ☐ ☐ ☐ ☐ ☐ ☐
Thursday	☐ ☐ ☐ ☐ ☐ ☐ ☐ ☐
Friday	☐ ☐ ☐ ☐ ☐ ☐ ☐ ☐
Saturday	☐ ☐ ☐ ☐ ☐ ☐ ☐ ☐
Sunday	☐ ☐ ☐ ☐ ☐ ☐ ☐ ☐

Daily Focus

What's The Priority?!

Monday
1.
2.
3.

Tuesday
1.
2.
3.

Wednesday
1.
2.
3.

Thursday
1.
2.
3.

Friday
1.
2.
3.

Saturday
1.
2.
3.

Sunday
1.
2.
3.

Moment Of Gratitude

This Week I Am Thankful For:

Notes:

The Week Of:

In Alignment With My Monthly Goals, This Week I Will Focus On:

1. Spiritual: _____
2. Physical/Health: _____
3. Family/Relationship: _____
4. Financial: _____
5. Personal: _____

Sub-Tasks:

_____
_____
_____
_____

My Consistency Tracker:

	Mon	Tue	Wed	Thu	Fri	Sat	Sun
_____							
_____							

My Water Consumption This Week (8x8oz Glasses Per-Day)

Monday	☐	☐	☐	☐	☐	☐	☐	☐
Tuesday	☐	☐	☐	☐	☐	☐	☐	☐
Wednesday	☐	☐	☐	☐	☐	☐	☐	☐
Thursday	☐	☐	☐	☐	☐	☐	☐	☐
Friday	☐	☐	☐	☐	☐	☐	☐	☐
Saturday	☐	☐	☐	☐	☐	☐	☐	☐
Sunday	☐	☐	☐	☐	☐	☐	☐	☐

Daily Focus

What's The Priority?!

Monday
1.
2.
3.

Tuesday
1.
2.
3.

Wednesday
1.
2.
3.

Thursday
1.
2.
3.

Friday
1.
2.
3.

Saturday
1.
2.
3.

Sunday
1.
2.
3.

Moment Of Gratitude

This Week I Am Thankful For:

Notes:

The Week Of:

In Alignment With My Monthly Goals, This Week I Will Focus On:

1. Spiritual: _____
2. Physical/Health: _____
3. Family/Relationship: _____
4. Financial: _____
5. Personal: _____

Sub-Tasks:

_____
_____
_____
_____

My Consistency Tracker:

	Mon	Tue	Wed	Thu	Fri	Sat	Sun
_____							
_____	Mon	Tue	Wed	Thu	Fri	Sat	Sun

My Water Consumption This Week (8x8oz Glasses Per-Day)

Monday	☐	☐	☐	☐	☐	☐	☐	☐
Tuesday	☐	☐	☐	☐	☐	☐	☐	☐
Wednesday	☐	☐	☐	☐	☐	☐	☐	☐
Thursday	☐	☐	☐	☐	☐	☐	☐	☐
Friday	☐	☐	☐	☐	☐	☐	☐	☐
Saturday	☐	☐	☐	☐	☐	☐	☐	☐
Sunday	☐	☐	☐	☐	☐	☐	☐	☐

Daily Focus

What's The Priority?!

Monday
1.
2.
3.

Tuesday
1.
2.
3.

Wednesday
1.
2.
3.

Thursday
1.
2.
3.

Friday
1.
2.
3.

Saturday
1.
2.
3.

Sunday
1.
2.
3.

Moment Of Gratitude

This Week I Am Thankful For:

The Week Of:

In Alignment With My Monthly Goals, This Week I Will Focus On:

1. Spiritual: _____
2. Physical/Health: _____
3. Family/Relationship: _____
4. Financial: _____
5. Personal: _____

Sub-Tasks:

_____
_____
_____
_____

My Consistency Tracker:

_____	Mon	Tue	Wed	Thu	Fri	Sat	Sun
_____	Mon	Tue	Wed	Thu	Fri	Sat	Sun

My Water Consumption This Week (8x8oz Glasses Per-Day)

Monday	☐ ☐ ☐ ☐ ☐ ☐ ☐ ☐
Tuesday	☐ ☐ ☐ ☐ ☐ ☐ ☐ ☐
Wednesday	☐ ☐ ☐ ☐ ☐ ☐ ☐ ☐
Thursday	☐ ☐ ☐ ☐ ☐ ☐ ☐ ☐
Friday	☐ ☐ ☐ ☐ ☐ ☐ ☐ ☐
Saturday	☐ ☐ ☐ ☐ ☐ ☐ ☐ ☐
Sunday	☐ ☐ ☐ ☐ ☐ ☐ ☐ ☐

Daily Focus

What's The Priority?!

Monday
1.
2.
3.

Tuesday
1.
2.
3.

Wednesday
1.
2.
3.

Thursday
1.
2.
3.

Friday
1.
2.
3.

Saturday
1.
2.
3.

Sunday
1.
2.
3.

Moment Of Gratitude

This Week I Am Thankful For:

_____
_____
_____
_____
_____
_____
_____
_____
_____
_____
_____
_____
_____
_____
_____
_____
_____
_____
_____
_____
_____

Notes:

Monthly Recap

Reassess, Reset, Re-Focus

Reassess

This Month I Accomplished:

_____
_____
_____
_____
_____

I Allowed The Following Things To Distract Me:

_____
_____
_____
_____
_____

I Remained Consistent With:

_____
_____
_____
_____
_____

Monthly Recap

Reassess, Reset, Re-Focus

My Overall Assessment Of This Month:

_____

_____

_____

_____

_____

_____

_____

Reset
Next Month I Will Focus More On:

_____

_____

_____

_____

_____

_____

_____

Re-Focus
Review Your Yearly Goals And Your Why Statement To Keep You In-Focus Before Moving Into The Next Month.

Month:

My Goals This Month, In Alignment With My Yearly Goals Are:

1. Spiritual: _____
2. Physical/Health: _____
3. Family/Relationship: _____
4. Financial: _____
5. Personal: _____

I Will Accomplish These Goals By Doing The Following Things This Month:

_____
_____
_____
_____
_____
_____
_____
_____
_____
_____
_____
_____

I Want To Remain Consistent With The Following Things This Month:

1. _____
2. _____

Tag Us On Instagram: @SheHasGoalsJournal

The Week Of:

In Alignment With My Monthly Goals, This Week I Will Focus On

3. Spiritual: _____
4. Physical/Health: _____
5. Family/Relationship: _____
6. Financial: _____
7. Personal: _____

Sub-Tasks:

_____
_____
_____
_____

My Consistency Tracker:

| _____ | Mon | Tue | Wed | Thu | Fri | Sat | Sun |
| _____ | Mon | Tue | Wed | Thu | Fri | Sat | Sun |

My Water Consumption This Week (8x8oz Glasses Per-Day)

Monday	☐	☐	☐	☐	☐	☐	☐	☐
Tuesday	☐	☐	☐	☐	☐	☐	☐	☐
Wednesday	☐	☐	☐	☐	☐	☐	☐	☐
Thursday	☐	☐	☐	☐	☐	☐	☐	☐
Friday	☐	☐	☐	☐	☐	☐	☐	☐
Saturday	☐	☐	☐	☐	☐	☐	☐	☐
Sunday	☐	☐	☐	☐	☐	☐	☐	☐

Daily Focus

What's The Priority?!

Monday
1.
2.
3.

Tuesday
1.
2.
3.

Wednesday
1.
2.
3.

Thursday
1.
2.
3.

Friday
1.
2.
3.

Saturday
1.
2.
3.

Sunday
1.
2.
3.

Moment Of Gratitude

This Week I Am Thankful For:

Notes:

The Week Of:

In Alignment With My Monthly Goals, This Week I Will Focus On:

1. Spiritual: _____
2. Physical/Health: _____
3. Family/Relationship: _____
4. Financial: _____
5. Personal: _____

Sub-Tasks:

_____

_____

_____

_____

My Consistency Tracker:

_____ | Mon | Tue | Wed | Thu | Fri | Sat | Sun |

_____ | Mon | Tue | Wed | Thu | Fri | Sat | Sun |

My Water Consumption This Week (8x8oz Glasses Per-Day)

Monday	☐	☐	☐	☐	☐	☐	☐	☐
Tuesday	☐	☐	☐	☐	☐	☐	☐	☐
Wednesday	☐	☐	☐	☐	☐	☐	☐	☐
Thursday	☐	☐	☐	☐	☐	☐	☐	☐
Friday	☐	☐	☐	☐	☐	☐	☐	☐
Saturday	☐	☐	☐	☐	☐	☐	☐	☐
Sunday	☐	☐	☐	☐	☐	☐	☐	☐

Daily Focus

What's The Priority?!

Monday
1.
2.
3.

Tuesday
1.
2.
3.

Wednesday
1.
2.
3.

Thursday
1.
2.
3.

Friday
1.
2.
3.

Saturday
1.
2.
3.

Sunday
1.
2.
3.

Moment Of Gratitude

This Week I Am Thankful For:

Notes:

The Week Of:

In Alignment With My Monthly Goals, This Week I Will Focus On:

1. Spiritual: _____
2. Physical/Health: _____
3. Family/Relationship: _____
4. Financial: _____
5. Personal: _____

Sub-Tasks:

_____
_____
_____
_____

My Consistency Tracker:

_____	Mon	Tue	Wed	Thu	Fri	Sat	Sun
_____	Mon	Tue	Wed	Thu	Fri	Sat	Sun

My Water Consumption This Week (8x8oz Glasses Per-Day)

Monday	☐	☐	☐	☐	☐	☐	☐	☐
Tuesday	☐	☐	☐	☐	☐	☐	☐	☐
Wednesday	☐	☐	☐	☐	☐	☐	☐	☐
Thursday	☐	☐	☐	☐	☐	☐	☐	☐
Friday	☐	☐	☐	☐	☐	☐	☐	☐
Saturday	☐	☐	☐	☐	☐	☐	☐	☐
Sunday	☐	☐	☐	☐	☐	☐	☐	☐

Daily Focus

What's The Priority?!

Monday
1.
2.
3.

Tuesday
1.
2.
3.

Wednesday
1.
2.
3.

Thursday
1.
2.
3.

Friday
1.
2.
3.

Saturday
1.
2.
3.

Sunday
1.
2.
3.

Moment Of Gratitude

This Week I Am Thankful For:

Notes:

The Week Of:

In Alignment With My Monthly Goals, This Week I Will Focus On:

1. Spiritual:_____
2. Physical/Health: _____
3. Family/Relationship: _____
4. Financial: _____
5. Personal: _____

Sub-Tasks:

_____
_____
_____
_____

My Consistency Tracker:

| _____ | Mon | Tue | Wed | Thu | Fri | Sat | Sun |
| _____ | Mon | Tue | Wed | Thu | Fri | Sat | Sun |

My Water Consumption This Week (8x8oz Glasses Per-Day)

Monday	☐	☐	☐	☐	☐	☐	☐	☐
Tuesday	☐	☐	☐	☐	☐	☐	☐	☐
Wednesday	☐	☐	☐	☐	☐	☐	☐	☐
Thursday	☐	☐	☐	☐	☐	☐	☐	☐
Friday	☐	☐	☐	☐	☐	☐	☐	☐
Saturday	☐	☐	☐	☐	☐	☐	☐	☐
Sunday	☐	☐	☐	☐	☐	☐	☐	☐

Daily Focus

What's The Priority?!

Monday
1.
2.
3.

Tuesday
1.
2.
3.

Wednesday
1.
2.
3.

Thursday
1.
2.
3.

Friday
1.
2.
3.

Saturday
1.
2.
3.

Sunday
1.
2.
3.

Moment Of Gratitude

This Week I Am Thankful For:

Notes:

Monthly Recap

Reassess, Reset, Re-Focus

Reassess

This Month I Accomplished:

_____
_____
_____
_____
_____

I Allowed The Following Things To Distract Me:

_____
_____
_____
_____
_____

I Remained Consistent With:

_____
_____
_____
_____
_____

Monthly Recap

Reassess, Reset, Re-Focus

My Overall Assessment Of This Month:

_____

_____

_____

_____

_____

_____

_____

Reset
Next Month I Will Focus More On:

_____

_____

_____

_____

_____

_____

_____

Re-Focus
Review Your Yearly Goals And Your Why Statement To Keep You In-Focus Before Moving Into The Next Month.

Month:

My Goals This Month, In Alignment With My Yearly Goals Are:

1. Spiritual: _____
2. Physical/Health: _____
3. Family/Relationship: _____
4. Financial: _____
5. Personal: _____

I Will Accomplish These Goals By Doing The Following Things This Month:

_____
_____
_____
_____
_____
_____
_____
_____
_____
_____

I Want To Remain Consistent With The Following Things This Month:

1. _____
2. _____

Tag Us On Instagram: @SheHasGoalsJournal

The Week Of:

In Alignment With My Monthly Goals, This Week I Will Focus On:

1. Spiritual: _____
2. Physical/Health: _____
3. Family/Relationship: _____
4. Financial: _____
5. Personal: _____

Sub-Tasks:

_____
_____
_____
_____

My Consistency Tracker:

	Mon	Tue	Wed	Thu	Fri	Sat	Sun
_____							
_____							

My Water Consumption This Week (8x8oz Glasses Per-Day)

Monday	☐	☐	☐	☐	☐	☐	☐	☐
Tuesday	☐	☐	☐	☐	☐	☐	☐	☐
Wednesday	☐	☐	☐	☐	☐	☐	☐	☐
Thursday	☐	☐	☐	☐	☐	☐	☐	☐
Friday	☐	☐	☐	☐	☐	☐	☐	☐
Saturday	☐	☐	☐	☐	☐	☐	☐	☐
Sunday	☐	☐	☐	☐	☐	☐	☐	☐

Daily Focus

What's The Priority?!

Monday
1.
2.
3.

Tuesday
1.
2.
3.

Wednesday
1.
2.
3.

Thursday
1.
2.
3.

Friday
1.
2.
3.

Saturday
1.
2.
3.

Sunday
1.
2.
3.

Moment Of Gratitude

This Week I Am Thankful For:

Notes:

The Week Of:

In Alignment With My Monthly Goals, This Week I Will Focus On:

1. Spiritual: _____
2. Physical/Health: _____
3. Family/Relationship: _____
4. Financial: _____
5. Personal: _____

Sub-Tasks:

_____
_____
_____
_____

My Consistency Tracker:

	Mon	Tue	Wed	Thu	Fri	Sat	Sun
_____							
_____							

My Water Consumption This Week (8x8oz Glasses Per-Day)

Monday	☐	☐	☐	☐	☐	☐	☐	☐
Tuesday	☐	☐	☐	☐	☐	☐	☐	☐
Wednesday	☐	☐	☐	☐	☐	☐	☐	☐
Thursday	☐	☐	☐	☐	☐	☐	☐	☐
Friday	☐	☐	☐	☐	☐	☐	☐	☐
Saturday	☐	☐	☐	☐	☐	☐	☐	☐
Sunday	☐	☐	☐	☐	☐	☐	☐	☐

Daily Focus

What's The Priority?!

Monday
1.
2.
3.

Tuesday
1.
2.
3.

Wednesday
1.
2.
3.

Thursday
1.
2.
3.

Friday
1.
2.
3.

Saturday
1.
2.
3.

Sunday
1.
2.
3.

Moment Of Gratitude

This Week I Am Thankful For:

Notes:

The Week Of:

In Alignment With My Monthly Goals, This Week I Will Focus On:

1. Spiritual: _____
2. Physical/Health: _____
3. Family/Relationship: _____
4. Financial: _____
5. Personal: _____

Sub-Tasks:

_____
_____
_____
_____

My Consistency Tracker:

| _____ | Mon | Tue | Wed | Thu | Fri | Sat | Sun |
| _____ | Mon | Tue | Wed | Thu | Fri | Sat | Sun |

My Water Consumption This Week (8x8oz Glasses Per-Day)

Monday	☐ ☐ ☐ ☐ ☐ ☐ ☐ ☐
Tuesday	☐ ☐ ☐ ☐ ☐ ☐ ☐ ☐
Wednesday	☐ ☐ ☐ ☐ ☐ ☐ ☐ ☐
Thursday	☐ ☐ ☐ ☐ ☐ ☐ ☐ ☐
Friday	☐ ☐ ☐ ☐ ☐ ☐ ☐ ☐
Saturday	☐ ☐ ☐ ☐ ☐ ☐ ☐ ☐
Sunday	☐ ☐ ☐ ☐ ☐ ☐ ☐ ☐

Daily Focus

What's The Priority?!

Monday
1.
2.
3.

Tuesday
1.
2.
3.

Wednesday
1.
2.
3.

Thursday
1.
2.
3.

Friday
1.
2.
3.

Saturday
1.
2.
3.

Sunday
1.
2.
3.

Moment Of Gratitude

This Week I Am Thankful For:

_____
_____
_____
_____
_____
_____
_____
_____
_____
_____
_____
_____
_____
_____
_____
_____
_____
_____
_____
_____
_____
_____
_____

Notes:

The Week Of:

In Alignment With My Monthly Goals, This Week I Will Focus On:

1. Spiritual: _____
2. Physical/Health: _____
3. Family/Relationship: _____
4. Financial: _____
5. Personal: _____

Sub-Tasks:

_____
_____
_____
_____

My Consistency Tracker:

_____ | Mon | Tue | Wed | Thu | Fri | Sat | Sun |
_____ | Mon | Tue | Wed | Thu | Fri | Sat | Sun |

My Water Consumption This Week (8x8oz Glasses Per-Day)

Monday   ☐ ☐ ☐ ☐ ☐ ☐ ☐ ☐
Tuesday   ☐ ☐ ☐ ☐ ☐ ☐ ☐ ☐
Wednesday ☐ ☐ ☐ ☐ ☐ ☐ ☐ ☐
Thursday ☐ ☐ ☐ ☐ ☐ ☐ ☐ ☐
Friday   ☐ ☐ ☐ ☐ ☐ ☐ ☐ ☐
Saturday ☐ ☐ ☐ ☐ ☐ ☐ ☐ ☐
Sunday   ☐ ☐ ☐ ☐ ☐ ☐ ☐ ☐

Daily Focus

What's The Priority?!

Monday
1.
2.
3.

Tuesday
1.
2.
3.

Wednesday
1.
2.
3.

Thursday
1.
2.
3.

Friday
1.
2.
3.

Saturday
1.
2.
3.

Sunday
1.
2.
3.

Moment Of Gratitude

This Week I Am Thankful For:

Notes:

Monthly Recap

Reassess, Reset, Re-Focus

Reassess
This Month I Accomplished:

_____

_____

_____

_____

_____

I Allowed The Following Things To Distract Me:

_____

_____

_____

_____

_____

I Remained Consistent With:

_____

_____

_____

_____

_____

Monthly Recap

Reassess, Reset, Re-Focus

My Overall Assessment Of This Month:

_____

_____

_____

_____

_____

_____

_____

Reset
Next Month I Will Focus More On:

_____

_____

_____

_____

_____

_____

_____

Re-Focus
Review Your Yearly Goals And Your Why Statement To Keep You In-Focus Before Moving Into The Next Month.

Month: _____

My Goals This Month, In Alignment With My Yearly Goals Are:

1. Spiritual: _____
2. Physical/Health: _____
3. Family/Relationship: _____
4. Financial: _____
5. Personal: _____

I Will Accomplish These Goals By Doing The Following Things This Month:

_____
_____
_____
_____
_____
_____
_____
_____
_____
_____
_____

I Want To Remain Consistent With The Following Things This Month:

1. _____
2. _____

Tag Us On Instagram: @SheHasGoalsJournal

The Week Of:

In Alignment With My Monthly Goals, This Week I Will Focus On

3. Spiritual: _____

4. Physical/Health: _____

5. Family/Relationship: _____

6. Financial: _____

7. Personal: _____

Sub-Tasks:

_____

_____

_____

_____

My Consistency Tracker:

| _____ | Mon | Tue | Wed | Thu | Fri | Sat | Sun |
| _____ | Mon | Tue | Wed | Thu | Fri | Sat | Sun |

My Water Consumption This Week (8x8oz Glasses Per-Day)

Monday	☐ ☐ ☐ ☐ ☐ ☐ ☐ ☐
Tuesday	☐ ☐ ☐ ☐ ☐ ☐ ☐ ☐
Wednesday	☐ ☐ ☐ ☐ ☐ ☐ ☐ ☐
Thursday	☐ ☐ ☐ ☐ ☐ ☐ ☐ ☐
Friday	☐ ☐ ☐ ☐ ☐ ☐ ☐ ☐
Saturday	☐ ☐ ☐ ☐ ☐ ☐ ☐ ☐
Sunday	☐ ☐ ☐ ☐ ☐ ☐ ☐ ☐

Daily Focus

What's The Priority?!

Monday
1.
2.
3.

Tuesday
1.
2.
3.

Wednesday
1.
2.
3.

Thursday
1.
2.
3.

Friday
1.
2.
3.

Saturday
1.
2.
3.

Sunday
1.
2.
3.

Moment Of Gratitude

This Week I Am Thankful For:

Notes:

The Week Of:

In Alignment With My Monthly Goals, This Week I Will Focus On:

1. Spiritual: _____
2. Physical/Health: _____
3. Family/Relationship: _____
4. Financial: _____
5. Personal: _____

Sub-Tasks:

_____
_____
_____
_____

My Consistency Tracker:

	Mon	Tue	Wed	Thu	Fri	Sat	Sun
_____							
_____							

My Water Consumption This Week (8x8oz Glasses Per-Day)

Monday	☐	☐	☐	☐	☐	☐	☐	☐
Tuesday	☐	☐	☐	☐	☐	☐	☐	☐
Wednesday	☐	☐	☐	☐	☐	☐	☐	☐
Thursday	☐	☐	☐	☐	☐	☐	☐	☐
Friday	☐	☐	☐	☐	☐	☐	☐	☐
Saturday	☐	☐	☐	☐	☐	☐	☐	☐
Sunday	☐	☐	☐	☐	☐	☐	☐	☐

Daily Focus

What's The Priority?!

Monday
1.
2.
3.

Tuesday
1.
2.
3.

Wednesday
1.
2.
3.

Thursday
1.
2.
3.

Friday
1.
2.
3.

Saturday
1.
2.
3.

Sunday
1.
2.
3.

Moment Of Gratitude

This Week I Am Thankful For:

Notes:

The Week Of:

In Alignment With My Monthly Goals, This Week I Will Focus On:

1. Spiritual: _____
2. Physical/Health: _____
3. Family/Relationship: _____
4. Financial: _____
5. Personal: _____

Sub-Tasks:

_____
_____
_____
_____

My Consistency Tracker:

| _____ | Mon | Tue | Wed | Thu | Fri | Sat | Sun |
| _____ | Mon | Tue | Wed | Thu | Fri | Sat | Sun |

My Water Consumption This Week (8x8oz Glasses Per-Day)

Monday   ☐ ☐ ☐ ☐ ☐ ☐ ☐ ☐
Tuesday   ☐ ☐ ☐ ☐ ☐ ☐ ☐ ☐
Wednesday   ☐ ☐ ☐ ☐ ☐ ☐ ☐ ☐
Thursday   ☐ ☐ ☐ ☐ ☐ ☐ ☐ ☐
Friday   ☐ ☐ ☐ ☐ ☐ ☐ ☐ ☐
Saturday   ☐ ☐ ☐ ☐ ☐ ☐ ☐ ☐
Sunday   ☐ ☐ ☐ ☐ ☐ ☐ ☐ ☐

Daily Focus

What's The Priority?!

Monday
1.
2.
3.

Tuesday
1.
2.
3.

Wednesday
1.
2.
3.

Thursday
1.
2.
3.

Friday
1.
2.
3.

Saturday
1.
2.
3.

Sunday
1.
2.
3.

Moment Of Gratitude

This Week I Am Thankful For:

Notes:

The Week Of:

In Alignment With My Monthly Goals, This Week I Will Focus On:

1. Spiritual: _____
2. Physical/Health: _____
3. Family/Relationship: _____
4. Financial: _____
5. Personal: _____

Sub-Tasks:

_____
_____
_____
_____

My Consistency Tracker:

	Mon	Tue	Wed	Thu	Fri	Sat	Sun
_____	☐	☐	☐	☐	☐	☐	☐
_____	☐	☐	☐	☐	☐	☐	☐

My Water Consumption This Week (8x8oz Glasses Per-Day)

Monday	☐	☐	☐	☐	☐	☐	☐	☐
Tuesday	☐	☐	☐	☐	☐	☐	☐	☐
Wednesday	☐	☐	☐	☐	☐	☐	☐	☐
Thursday	☐	☐	☐	☐	☐	☐	☐	☐
Friday	☐	☐	☐	☐	☐	☐	☐	☐
Saturday	☐	☐	☐	☐	☐	☐	☐	☐
Sunday	☐	☐	☐	☐	☐	☐	☐	☐

Daily Focus

What's The Priority?!

Monday
1.
2.
3.

Tuesday
1.
2.
3.

Wednesday
1.
2.
3.

Thursday
1.
2.
3.

Friday
1.
2.
3.

Saturday
1.
2.
3.

Sunday
1.
2.
3.

Moment Of Gratitude

This Week I Am Thankful For:

Notes:

Monthly Recap

Reassess, Reset, Re-Focus

Reassess

This Month I Accomplished:

_____

_____

_____

_____

_____

I Allowed The Following Things To Distract Me:

_____

_____

_____

_____

_____

I Remained Consistent With:

_____

_____

_____

_____

_____

Monthly Recap

Reassess, Reset, Re-Focus

My Overall Assessment Of This Month:

_____
_____
_____
_____
_____
_____
_____

Reset
Next Month I Will Focus More On:

_____
_____
_____
_____
_____
_____
_____

Re-Focus
Review Your Yearly Goals And Your Why Statement To Keep You In-Focus Before Moving Into The Next Month.

Month: _____

My Goals This Month, In Alignment With My Yearly Goals Are:

1. Spiritual: _____
2. Physical/Health: _____
3. Family/Relationship: _____
4. Financial: _____
5. Personal: _____

I Will Accomplish These Goals By Doing The Following Things This Month:

_____
_____
_____
_____
_____
_____
_____
_____
_____
_____
_____

I Want To Remain Consistent With The Following Things This Month:

1. _____
2. _____

Tag Us On Instagram: @SheHasGoalsJournal

The Week Of:

In Alignment With My Monthly Goals, This Week I Will Focus On:

1. Spiritual: _____
2. Physical/Health: _____
3. Family/Relationship: _____
4. Financial: _____
5. Personal: _____

Sub-Tasks:

_____
_____
_____
_____

My Consistency Tracker:

| _____ | Mon | Tue | Wed | Thu | Fri | Sat | Sun |
| _____ | Mon | Tue | Wed | Thu | Fri | Sat | Sun |

My Water Consumption This Week (8x8oz Glasses Per-Day)

Monday	☐ ☐ ☐ ☐ ☐ ☐ ☐ ☐
Tuesday	☐ ☐ ☐ ☐ ☐ ☐ ☐ ☐
Wednesday	☐ ☐ ☐ ☐ ☐ ☐ ☐ ☐
Thursday	☐ ☐ ☐ ☐ ☐ ☐ ☐ ☐
Friday	☐ ☐ ☐ ☐ ☐ ☐ ☐ ☐
Saturday	☐ ☐ ☐ ☐ ☐ ☐ ☐ ☐
Sunday	☐ ☐ ☐ ☐ ☐ ☐ ☐ ☐

Daily Focus

What's The Priority?!

Monday
1.
2.
3.

Tuesday
1.
2.
3.

Wednesday
1.
2.
3.

Thursday
1.
2.
3.

Friday
1.
2.
3.

Saturday
1.
2.
3.

Sunday
1.
2.
3.

Moment Of Gratitude

This Week I Am Thankful For:

Notes:

The Week Of:

In Alignment With My Monthly Goals, This Week I Will Focus On:

1. Spiritual: _____
2. Physical/Health: _____
3. Family/Relationship: _____
4. Financial: _____
5. Personal: _____

Sub-Tasks:

_____
_____
_____
_____

My Consistency Tracker:

| _____ | Mon | Tue | Wed | Thu | Fri | Sat | Sun |
| _____ | Mon | Tue | Wed | Thu | Fri | Sat | Sun |

My Water Consumption This Week (8x8oz Glasses Per-Day)

Monday ☐ ☐ ☐ ☐ ☐ ☐ ☐ ☐
Tuesday ☐ ☐ ☐ ☐ ☐ ☐ ☐ ☐
Wednesday ☐ ☐ ☐ ☐ ☐ ☐ ☐ ☐
Thursday ☐ ☐ ☐ ☐ ☐ ☐ ☐ ☐
Friday ☐ ☐ ☐ ☐ ☐ ☐ ☐ ☐
Saturday ☐ ☐ ☐ ☐ ☐ ☐ ☐ ☐
Sunday ☐ ☐ ☐ ☐ ☐ ☐ ☐ ☐

Daily Focus

What's The Priority?!

Monday
1.
2.
3.

Tuesday
1.
2.
3.

Wednesday
1.
2.
3.

Thursday
1.
2.
3.

Friday
1.
2.
3.

Saturday
1.
2.
3.

Sunday
1.
2.
3.

Moment Of Gratitude

This Week I Am Thankful For:

Notes:

The Week Of:

In Alignment With My Monthly Goals, This Week I Will Focus On:

1. Spiritual: _____
2. Physical/Health: _____
3. Family/Relationship: _____
4. Financial: _____
5. Personal: _____

Sub-Tasks:

_____
_____
_____
_____

My Consistency Tracker:

	Mon	Tue	Wed	Thu	Fri	Sat	Sun
_____							
_____							

My Water Consumption This Week (8x8oz Glasses Per-Day)

Monday	☐	☐	☐	☐	☐	☐	☐	☐
Tuesday	☐	☐	☐	☐	☐	☐	☐	☐
Wednesday	☐	☐	☐	☐	☐	☐	☐	☐
Thursday	☐	☐	☐	☐	☐	☐	☐	☐
Friday	☐	☐	☐	☐	☐	☐	☐	☐
Saturday	☐	☐	☐	☐	☐	☐	☐	☐
Sunday	☐	☐	☐	☐	☐	☐	☐	☐

Daily Focus

What's The Priority?!

Monday
1.
2.
3.

Tuesday
1.
2.
3.

Wednesday
1.
2.
3.

Thursday
1.
2.
3.

Friday
1.
2.
3.

Saturday
1.
2.
3.

Sunday
1.
2.
3.

Moment Of Gratitude

This Week I Am Thankful For:

Notes:

The Week Of:

In Alignment With My Monthly Goals, This Week I Will Focus On:

1. Spiritual: _____
2. Physical/Health: _____
3. Family/Relationship: _____
4. Financial: _____
5. Personal: _____

Sub-Tasks:

_____
_____
_____
_____

My Consistency Tracker:

| _____ | Mon | Tue | Wed | Thu | Fri | Sat | Sun |
| _____ | Mon | Tue | Wed | Thu | Fri | Sat | Sun |

My Water Consumption This Week (8x8oz Glasses Per-Day)

Monday	☐ ☐ ☐ ☐ ☐ ☐ ☐ ☐
Tuesday	☐ ☐ ☐ ☐ ☐ ☐ ☐ ☐
Wednesday	☐ ☐ ☐ ☐ ☐ ☐ ☐ ☐
Thursday	☐ ☐ ☐ ☐ ☐ ☐ ☐ ☐
Friday	☐ ☐ ☐ ☐ ☐ ☐ ☐ ☐
Saturday	☐ ☐ ☐ ☐ ☐ ☐ ☐ ☐
Sunday	☐ ☐ ☐ ☐ ☐ ☐ ☐ ☐

Daily Focus

What's The Priority?!

Monday
1.
2.
3.

Tuesday
1.
2.
3.

Wednesday
1.
2.
3.

Thursday
1.
2.
3.

Friday
1.
2.
3.

Saturday
1.
2.
3.

Sunday
1.
2.
3.

Moment Of Gratitude

This Week I Am Thankful For:

_____
_____
_____
_____
_____
_____
_____
_____
_____
_____
_____
_____
_____
_____
_____
_____
_____
_____
_____
_____
_____
_____

Notes:

Monthly Recap

Reassess, Reset, Re-Focus

Reassess

This Month I Accomplished:

_____
_____
_____
_____
_____

I Allowed The Following Things To Distract Me:

_____
_____
_____
_____
_____

I Remained Consistent With:

_____
_____
_____
_____
_____

Monthly Recap

Reassess, Reset, Re-Focus

My Overall Assessment Of This Month:

_____

_____

_____

_____

_____

_____

_____

Reset
Next Month I Will Focus More On:

_____

_____

_____

_____

_____

_____

_____

Re-Focus
Review Your Yearly Goals And Your Why Statement To Keep You In-Focus Before Moving Into The Next Month.

Month:

My Goals This Month, In Alignment With My Yearly Goals Are:

1. Spiritual: _____
2. Physical/Health: _____
3. Family/Relationship: _____
4. Financial: _____
5. Personal: _____

I Will Accomplish These Goals By Doing The Following Things This Month:

_____
_____
_____
_____
_____
_____
_____
_____
_____
_____
_____
_____

I Want To Remain Consistent With The Following Things This Month:

1. _____
2. _____

Tag Us On Instagram: @SheHasGoalsJournal

The Week Of:

In Alignment With My Monthly Goals, This Week I Will Focus On

3. Spiritual: _____

4. Physical/Health: _____

5. Family/Relationship: _____

6. Financial: _____

7. Personal: _____

Sub-Tasks:

_____

_____

_____

_____

My Consistency Tracker:

_____ | Mon | Tue | Wed | Thu | Fri | Sat | Sun |

_____ | Mon | Tue | Wed | Thu | Fri | Sat | Sun |

My Water Consumption This Week (8x8oz Glasses Per-Day)

Monday	☐	☐	☐	☐	☐	☐	☐	☐
Tuesday	☐	☐	☐	☐	☐	☐	☐	☐
Wednesday	☐	☐	☐	☐	☐	☐	☐	☐
Thursday	☐	☐	☐	☐	☐	☐	☐	☐
Friday	☐	☐	☐	☐	☐	☐	☐	☐
Saturday	☐	☐	☐	☐	☐	☐	☐	☐
Sunday	☐	☐	☐	☐	☐	☐	☐	☐

Daily Focus

What's The Priority?!

Monday
1.
2.
3.

Tuesday
1.
2.
3.

Wednesday
1.
2.
3.

Thursday
1.
2.
3.

Friday
1.
2.
3.

Saturday
1.
2.
3.

Sunday
1.
2.
3.

Moment Of Gratitude

This Week I Am Thankful For:

Notes:

The Week Of:

In Alignment With My Monthly Goals, This Week I Will Focus On:

1. Spiritual: _____
2. Physical/Health: _____
3. Family/Relationship: _____
4. Financial: _____
5. Personal: _____

Sub-Tasks:

_____

_____

_____

_____

My Consistency Tracker:

| _____ | Mon | Tue | Wed | Thu | Fri | Sat | Sun |
| _____ | Mon | Tue | Wed | Thu | Fri | Sat | Sun |

My Water Consumption This Week (8x8oz Glasses Per-Day)

Monday	☐ ☐ ☐ ☐ ☐ ☐ ☐ ☐
Tuesday	☐ ☐ ☐ ☐ ☐ ☐ ☐ ☐
Wednesday	☐ ☐ ☐ ☐ ☐ ☐ ☐ ☐
Thursday	☐ ☐ ☐ ☐ ☐ ☐ ☐ ☐
Friday	☐ ☐ ☐ ☐ ☐ ☐ ☐ ☐
Saturday	☐ ☐ ☐ ☐ ☐ ☐ ☐ ☐
Sunday	☐ ☐ ☐ ☐ ☐ ☐ ☐ ☐

Daily Focus

What's The Priority?!

Monday
1.
2.
3.

Tuesday
1.
2.
3.

Wednesday
1.
2.
3.

Thursday
1.
2.
3.

Friday
1.
2.
3.

Saturday
1.
2.
3.

Sunday
1.
2.
3.

Moment Of Gratitude

This Week I Am Thankful For:

Notes:

The Week Of:

In Alignment With My Monthly Goals, This Week I Will Focus On:

1. Spiritual: _____
2. Physical/Health: _____
3. Family/Relationship: _____
4. Financial: _____
5. Personal: _____

Sub-Tasks:

_____
_____
_____
_____

My Consistency Tracker:

| _____ | Mon | Tue | Wed | Thu | Fri | Sat | Sun |
| _____ | Mon | Tue | Wed | Thu | Fri | Sat | Sun |

My Water Consumption This Week (8x8oz Glasses Per-Day)

Monday	☐ ☐ ☐ ☐ ☐ ☐ ☐ ☐
Tuesday	☐ ☐ ☐ ☐ ☐ ☐ ☐ ☐
Wednesday	☐ ☐ ☐ ☐ ☐ ☐ ☐ ☐
Thursday	☐ ☐ ☐ ☐ ☐ ☐ ☐ ☐
Friday	☐ ☐ ☐ ☐ ☐ ☐ ☐ ☐
Saturday	☐ ☐ ☐ ☐ ☐ ☐ ☐ ☐
Sunday	☐ ☐ ☐ ☐ ☐ ☐ ☐ ☐

Daily Focus

What's The Priority?!

Monday
1.
2.
3.

Tuesday
1.
2.
3.

Wednesday
1.
2.
3.

Thursday
1.
2.
3.

Friday
1.
2.
3.

Saturday
1.
2.
3.

Sunday
1.
2.
3.

Moment Of Gratitude

This Week I Am Thankful For:

_____
_____
_____
_____
_____
_____
_____
_____
_____
_____
_____
_____
_____
_____
_____
_____
_____
_____
_____
_____
_____
_____

Notes:

The Week Of:

In Alignment With My Monthly Goals, This Week I Will Focus On:

1. Spiritual: _____
2. Physical/Health: _____
3. Family/Relationship: _____
4. Financial: _____
5. Personal: _____

Sub-Tasks:

_____
_____
_____
_____

My Consistency Tracker:

	Mon	Tue	Wed	Thu	Fri	Sat	Sun
_____							
_____	Mon	Tue	Wed	Thu	Fri	Sat	Sun

My Water Consumption This Week (8x8oz Glasses Per-Day)

Monday	☐	☐	☐	☐	☐	☐	☐	☐
Tuesday	☐	☐	☐	☐	☐	☐	☐	☐
Wednesday	☐	☐	☐	☐	☐	☐	☐	☐
Thursday	☐	☐	☐	☐	☐	☐	☐	☐
Friday	☐	☐	☐	☐	☐	☐	☐	☐
Saturday	☐	☐	☐	☐	☐	☐	☐	☐
Sunday	☐	☐	☐	☐	☐	☐	☐	☐

Daily Focus

What's The Priority?!

Monday
1.
2.
3.

Tuesday
1.
2.
3.

Wednesday
1.
2.
3.

Thursday
1.
2.
3.

Friday
1.
2.
3.

Saturday
1.
2.
3.

Sunday
1.
2.
3.

Moment Of Gratitude

This Week I Am Thankful For:

Notes:

Monthly Recap

Reassess, Reset, Re-Focus

Reassess

This Month I Accomplished:

_____
_____
_____
_____
_____
_____

I Allowed The Following Things To Distract Me:

_____
_____
_____
_____
_____
_____

I Remained Consistent With:

_____
_____
_____
_____
_____
_____

Monthly Recap

Reassess, Reset, Re-Focus

My Overall Assessment Of This Month:

_____
_____
_____
_____
_____
_____
_____

Reset
Next Month I Will Focus More On:

_____
_____
_____
_____
_____
_____
_____

Re-Focus
Review Your Yearly Goals And Your Why Statement To Keep You In-Focus Before Moving Into The Next Month.

Month: _____

My Goals This Month, In Alignment With My Yearly Goals Are:

1. Spiritual: _____
2. Physical/Health: _____
3. Family/Relationship: _____
4. Financial: _____
5. Personal: _____

I Will Accomplish These Goals By Doing The Following Things This Month:

_____
_____
_____
_____
_____
_____
_____
_____
_____
_____
_____

I Want To Remain Consistent With The Following Things This Month:

1. _____
2. _____

Tag Us On Instagram: @SheHasGoalsJournal

The Week Of:

In Alignment With My Monthly Goals, This Week I Will Focus On:

1. Spiritual: _____
2. Physical/Health: _____
3. Family/Relationship: _____
4. Financial: _____
5. Personal: _____

Sub-Tasks:

_____
_____
_____
_____

My Consistency Tracker:

_____	Mon	Tue	Wed	Thu	Fri	Sat	Sun
_____	Mon	Tue	Wed	Thu	Fri	Sat	Sun

My Water Consumption This Week (8x8oz Glasses Per-Day)

Monday	☐ ☐ ☐ ☐ ☐ ☐ ☐ ☐
Tuesday	☐ ☐ ☐ ☐ ☐ ☐ ☐ ☐
Wednesday	☐ ☐ ☐ ☐ ☐ ☐ ☐ ☐
Thursday	☐ ☐ ☐ ☐ ☐ ☐ ☐ ☐
Friday	☐ ☐ ☐ ☐ ☐ ☐ ☐ ☐
Saturday	☐ ☐ ☐ ☐ ☐ ☐ ☐ ☐
Sunday	☐ ☐ ☐ ☐ ☐ ☐ ☐ ☐

Daily Focus

What's The Priority?!

Monday
1.
2.
3.

Tuesday
1.
2.
3.

Wednesday
1.
2.
3.

Thursday
1.
2.
3.

Friday
1.
2.
3.

Saturday
1.
2.
3.

Sunday
1.
2.
3.

Moment Of Gratitude

This Week I Am Thankful For:

Notes:

The Week Of:

In Alignment With My Monthly Goals, This Week I Will Focus On:

1. Spiritual: _____
2. Physical/Health: _____
3. Family/Relationship: _____
4. Financial: _____
5. Personal: _____

Sub-Tasks:

_____
_____
_____
_____

My Consistency Tracker:

	Mon	Tue	Wed	Thu	Fri	Sat	Sun
_____							
_____							

My Water Consumption This Week (8x8oz Glasses Per-Day)

Monday ☐ ☐ ☐ ☐ ☐ ☐ ☐ ☐
Tuesday ☐ ☐ ☐ ☐ ☐ ☐ ☐ ☐
Wednesday ☐ ☐ ☐ ☐ ☐ ☐ ☐ ☐
Thursday ☐ ☐ ☐ ☐ ☐ ☐ ☐ ☐
Friday ☐ ☐ ☐ ☐ ☐ ☐ ☐ ☐
Saturday ☐ ☐ ☐ ☐ ☐ ☐ ☐ ☐
Sunday ☐ ☐ ☐ ☐ ☐ ☐ ☐ ☐

Daily Focus

What's The Priority?!

Monday
1.
2.
3.
___
Tuesday
1.
2.
3.
___
Wednesday
1.
2.
3.
___
Thursday
1.
2.
3.
___
Friday
1.
2.
3.
___
Saturday
1.
2.
3.
___
Sunday
1.
2.
3.

Moment Of Gratitude

This Week I Am Thankful For:

_____
_____
_____
_____
_____
_____
_____
_____
_____
_____
_____
_____
_____
_____
_____
_____
_____
_____
_____
_____
_____

Notes:

The Week Of:

In Alignment With My Monthly Goals, This Week I Will Focus On:

1. Spiritual: _____
2. Physical/Health: _____
3. Family/Relationship: _____
4. Financial: _____
5. Personal: _____

Sub-Tasks:

_____
_____
_____
_____

My Consistency Tracker:

	Mon	Tue	Wed	Thu	Fri	Sat	Sun
_____							
_____							

My Water Consumption This Week (8x8oz Glasses Per-Day)

Monday	☐	☐	☐	☐	☐	☐	☐	☐
Tuesday	☐	☐	☐	☐	☐	☐	☐	☐
Wednesday	☐	☐	☐	☐	☐	☐	☐	☐
Thursday	☐	☐	☐	☐	☐	☐	☐	☐
Friday	☐	☐	☐	☐	☐	☐	☐	☐
Saturday	☐	☐	☐	☐	☐	☐	☐	☐
Sunday	☐	☐	☐	☐	☐	☐	☐	☐

Daily Focus

What's The Priority?!

Monday
1.
2.
3.

Tuesday
1.
2.
3.

Wednesday
1.
2.
3.

Thursday
1.
2.
3.

Friday
1.
2.
3.

Saturday
1.
2.
3.

Sunday
1.
2.
3.

Moment Of Gratitude

This Week I Am Thankful For:

Notes:

The Week Of:

In Alignment With My Monthly Goals, This Week I Will Focus On:

1. Spiritual: _____
2. Physical/Health: _____
3. Family/Relationship: _____
4. Financial: _____
5. Personal: _____

Sub-Tasks:

_____
_____
_____
_____

My Consistency Tracker:

	Mon	Tue	Wed	Thu	Fri	Sat	Sun
_____							
_____							

My Water Consumption This Week (8x8oz Glasses Per-Day)

Monday	☐	☐	☐	☐	☐	☐	☐	☐
Tuesday	☐	☐	☐	☐	☐	☐	☐	☐
Wednesday	☐	☐	☐	☐	☐	☐	☐	☐
Thursday	☐	☐	☐	☐	☐	☐	☐	☐
Friday	☐	☐	☐	☐	☐	☐	☐	☐
Saturday	☐	☐	☐	☐	☐	☐	☐	☐
Sunday	☐	☐	☐	☐	☐	☐	☐	☐

Daily Focus

What's The Priority?!

Monday
1.
2.
3.

Tuesday
1.
2.
3.

Wednesday
1.
2.
3.

Thursday
1.
2.
3.

Friday
1.
2.
3.

Saturday
1.
2.
3.

Sunday
1.
2.
3.

Moment Of Gratitude

This Week I Am Thankful For:

Notes:

Monthly Recap

Reassess, Reset, Re-Focus

Reassess

This Month I Accomplished:

_____
_____
_____
_____
_____

I Allowed The Following Things To Distract Me:

_____
_____
_____
_____
_____

I Remained Consistent With:

_____
_____
_____
_____
_____

Monthly Recap

Reassess, Reset, Re-Focus

My Overall Assessment Of This Month:

_____

_____

_____

_____

_____

_____

_____

Reset
Next Month I Will Focus More On:

_____

_____

_____

_____

_____

_____

_____

Re-Focus
Review Your Yearly Goals And Your Why Statement To Keep You In-Focus Before Moving Into The Next Month.

Month: _____

My Goals This Month, In Alignment With My Yearly Goals Are:

1. Spiritual: _____
2. Physical/Health: _____
3. Family/Relationship: _____
4. Financial: _____
5. Personal: _____

I Will Accomplish These Goals By Doing The Following Things This Month:

_____
_____
_____
_____
_____
_____
_____
_____
_____
_____
_____
_____

I Want To Remain Consistent With The Following Things This Month:

1. _____
2. _____

Tag Us On Instagram: @SheHasGoalsJournal

The Week Of:

In Alignment With My Monthly Goals, This Week I Will Focus On

3. Spiritual: _____

4. Physical/Health: _____

5. Family/Relationship: _____

6. Financial: _____

7. Personal: _____

Sub-Tasks:

_____

_____

_____

_____

My Consistency Tracker:

	Mon	Tue	Wed	Thu	Fri	Sat	Sun
_____							
_____	Mon	Tue	Wed	Thu	Fri	Sat	Sun

My Water Consumption This Week (8x8oz Glasses Per-Day)

Monday	☐	☐	☐	☐	☐	☐	☐	☐
Tuesday	☐	☐	☐	☐	☐	☐	☐	☐
Wednesday	☐	☐	☐	☐	☐	☐	☐	☐
Thursday	☐	☐	☐	☐	☐	☐	☐	☐
Friday	☐	☐	☐	☐	☐	☐	☐	☐
Saturday	☐	☐	☐	☐	☐	☐	☐	☐
Sunday	☐	☐	☐	☐	☐	☐	☐	☐

| Daily Focus |

What's The Priority?!

Monday
1.
2.
3.

Tuesday
1.
2.
3.

Wednesday
1.
2.
3.

Thursday
1.
2.
3.

Friday
1.
2.
3.

Saturday
1.
2.
3.

Sunday
1.
2.
3.

Moment Of Gratitude

This Week I Am Thankful For:

Notes:

The Week Of:

In Alignment With My Monthly Goals, This Week I Will Focus On:

1. Spiritual: _____
2. Physical/Health: _____
3. Family/Relationship: _____
4. Financial: _____
5. Personal: _____

Sub-Tasks:

_____
_____
_____
_____

My Consistency Tracker:

| _____ | Mon | Tue | Wed | Thu | Fri | Sat | Sun |
| _____ | Mon | Tue | Wed | Thu | Fri | Sat | Sun |

My Water Consumption This Week (8x8oz Glasses Per-Day)

Monday	☐ ☐ ☐ ☐ ☐ ☐ ☐ ☐
Tuesday	☐ ☐ ☐ ☐ ☐ ☐ ☐ ☐
Wednesday	☐ ☐ ☐ ☐ ☐ ☐ ☐ ☐
Thursday	☐ ☐ ☐ ☐ ☐ ☐ ☐ ☐
Friday	☐ ☐ ☐ ☐ ☐ ☐ ☐ ☐
Saturday	☐ ☐ ☐ ☐ ☐ ☐ ☐ ☐
Sunday	☐ ☐ ☐ ☐ ☐ ☐ ☐ ☐

Daily Focus

What's The Priority?!

Monday
1.
2.
3.

Tuesday
1.
2.
3.

Wednesday
1.
2.
3.

Thursday
1.
2.
3.

Friday
1.
2.
3.

Saturday
1.
2.
3.

Sunday
1.
2.
3.

Moment Of Gratitude

This Week I Am Thankful For:

Notes:

The Week Of:

In Alignment With My Monthly Goals, This Week I Will Focus On:

1. Spiritual: _____
2. Physical/Health: _____
3. Family/Relationship: _____
4. Financial: _____
5. Personal: _____

Sub-Tasks:

_____

_____

_____

_____

My Consistency Tracker:

	Mon	Tue	Wed	Thu	Fri	Sat	Sun
	Mon	Tue	Wed	Thu	Fri	Sat	Sun

My Water Consumption This Week (8x8oz Glasses Per-Day)

Monday	☐	☐	☐	☐	☐	☐	☐	☐
Tuesday	☐	☐	☐	☐	☐	☐	☐	☐
Wednesday	☐	☐	☐	☐	☐	☐	☐	☐
Thursday	☐	☐	☐	☐	☐	☐	☐	☐
Friday	☐	☐	☐	☐	☐	☐	☐	☐
Saturday	☐	☐	☐	☐	☐	☐	☐	☐
Sunday	☐	☐	☐	☐	☐	☐	☐	☐

Daily Focus

What's The Priority?!

Monday
1.
2.
3.

Tuesday
1.
2.
3.

Wednesday
1.
2.
3.

Thursday
1.
2.
3.

Friday
1.
2.
3.

Saturday
1.
2.
3.

Sunday
1.
2.
3.

Moment Of Gratitude

This Week I Am Thankful For:

Notes:

The Week Of:

In Alignment With My Monthly Goals, This Week I Will Focus On:

1. Spiritual: _____
2. Physical/Health: _____
3. Family/Relationship: _____
4. Financial: _____
5. Personal: _____

Sub-Tasks:

_____
_____
_____
_____

My Consistency Tracker:

	Mon	Tue	Wed	Thu	Fri	Sat	Sun
_____							
_____							

My Water Consumption This Week (8x8oz Glasses Per-Day)

Monday	☐ ☐ ☐ ☐ ☐ ☐ ☐ ☐
Tuesday	☐ ☐ ☐ ☐ ☐ ☐ ☐ ☐
Wednesday	☐ ☐ ☐ ☐ ☐ ☐ ☐ ☐
Thursday	☐ ☐ ☐ ☐ ☐ ☐ ☐ ☐
Friday	☐ ☐ ☐ ☐ ☐ ☐ ☐ ☐
Saturday	☐ ☐ ☐ ☐ ☐ ☐ ☐ ☐
Sunday	☐ ☐ ☐ ☐ ☐ ☐ ☐ ☐

Daily Focus

What's The Priority?!

Monday
1.
2.
3.

Tuesday
1.
2.
3.

Wednesday
1.
2.
3.

Thursday
1.
2.
3.

Friday
1.
2.
3.

Saturday
1.
2.
3.

Sunday
1.
2.
3.

Moment Of Gratitude

This Week I Am Thankful For:

Notes:

Monthly Recap

Reassess, Reset, Re-Focus

Reassess

This Month I Accomplished:

_____

_____

_____

_____

_____

I Allowed The Following Things To Distract Me:

_____

_____

_____

_____

_____

I Remained Consistent With:

_____

_____

_____

_____

_____

Monthly Recap

Reassess, Reset, Re-Focus

My Overall Assessment Of This Month:

_____
_____
_____
_____
_____
_____
_____

Reset

Next Month I Will Focus More On:

_____
_____
_____
_____
_____
_____
_____

Re-Focus

Review Your Yearly Goals And Your Why Statement To Keep You In-Focus Before Moving Into The Next Month.

Month: _____

My Goals This Month, In Alignment With My Yearly Goals Are:

1. Spiritual: _____
2. Physical/Health: _____
3. Family/Relationship: _____
4. Financial: _____
5. Personal: _____

I Will Accomplish These Goals By Doing The Following Things This Month:

_____
_____
_____
_____
_____
_____
_____
_____
_____
_____

I Want To Remain Consistent With The Following Things This Month:

1. _____
2. _____

Tag Us On Instagram: @SheHasGoalsJournal

The Week Of:

In Alignment With My Monthly Goals, This Week I Will Focus On:

1. Spiritual: _____
2. Physical/Health: _____
3. Family/Relationship: _____
4. Financial: _____
5. Personal: _____

Sub-Tasks:

_____
_____
_____
_____

My Consistency Tracker:

_____ | Mon | Tue | Wed | Thu | Fri | Sat | Sun |
_____ | Mon | Tue | Wed | Thu | Fri | Sat | Sun |

My Water Consumption This Week (8x8oz Glasses Per-Day)

Monday   ☐ ☐ ☐ ☐ ☐ ☐ ☐ ☐
Tuesday   ☐ ☐ ☐ ☐ ☐ ☐ ☐ ☐
Wednesday ☐ ☐ ☐ ☐ ☐ ☐ ☐ ☐
Thursday   ☐ ☐ ☐ ☐ ☐ ☐ ☐ ☐
Friday   ☐ ☐ ☐ ☐ ☐ ☐ ☐ ☐
Saturday   ☐ ☐ ☐ ☐ ☐ ☐ ☐ ☐
Sunday   ☐ ☐ ☐ ☐ ☐ ☐ ☐ ☐

Daily Focus

What's The Priority?!

Monday
1.
2.
3.

Tuesday
1.
2.
3.

Wednesday
1.
2.
3.

Thursday
1.
2.
3.

Friday
1.
2.
3.

Saturday
1.
2.
3.

Sunday
1.
2.
3.

Moment Of Gratitude

This Week I Am Thankful For:

Notes:

The Week Of:

In Alignment With My Monthly Goals, This Week I Will Focus On:

1. Spiritual: _____
2. Physical/Health: _____
3. Family/Relationship: _____
4. Financial: _____
5. Personal: _____

Sub-Tasks:

_____
_____
_____
_____

My Consistency Tracker:

_____	Mon	Tue	Wed	Thu	Fri	Sat	Sun
_____	Mon	Tue	Wed	Thu	Fri	Sat	Sun

My Water Consumption This Week (8x8oz Glasses Per-Day)

Monday	☐ ☐ ☐ ☐ ☐ ☐ ☐ ☐
Tuesday	☐ ☐ ☐ ☐ ☐ ☐ ☐ ☐
Wednesday	☐ ☐ ☐ ☐ ☐ ☐ ☐ ☐
Thursday	☐ ☐ ☐ ☐ ☐ ☐ ☐ ☐
Friday	☐ ☐ ☐ ☐ ☐ ☐ ☐ ☐
Saturday	☐ ☐ ☐ ☐ ☐ ☐ ☐ ☐
Sunday	☐ ☐ ☐ ☐ ☐ ☐ ☐ ☐

Daily Focus

What's The Priority?!

Monday
1.
2.
3.

Tuesday
1.
2.
3.

Wednesday
1.
2.
3.

Thursday
1.
2.
3.

Friday
1.
2.
3.

Saturday
1.
2.
3.

Sunday
1.
2.
3.

Moment Of Gratitude

This Week I Am Thankful For:

Notes:

The Week Of:

In Alignment With My Monthly Goals, This Week I Will Focus On:

1. Spiritual: _____
2. Physical/Health: _____
3. Family/Relationship: _____
4. Financial: _____
5. Personal: _____

Sub-Tasks:

_____
_____
_____
_____

My Consistency Tracker:

	Mon	Tue	Wed	Thu	Fri	Sat	Sun

My Water Consumption This Week (8x8oz Glasses Per-Day)

Monday	☐ ☐ ☐ ☐ ☐ ☐ ☐ ☐
Tuesday	☐ ☐ ☐ ☐ ☐ ☐ ☐ ☐
Wednesday	☐ ☐ ☐ ☐ ☐ ☐ ☐ ☐
Thursday	☐ ☐ ☐ ☐ ☐ ☐ ☐ ☐
Friday	☐ ☐ ☐ ☐ ☐ ☐ ☐ ☐
Saturday	☐ ☐ ☐ ☐ ☐ ☐ ☐ ☐
Sunday	☐ ☐ ☐ ☐ ☐ ☐ ☐ ☐

Daily Focus

What's The Priority?!

Monday
1.
2.
3.

Tuesday
1.
2.
3.

Wednesday
1.
2.
3.

Thursday
1.
2.
3.

Friday
1.
2.
3.

Saturday
1.
2.
3.

Sunday
1.
2.
3.

Moment Of Gratitude

This Week I Am Thankful For:

Notes:

The Week Of:

In Alignment With My Monthly Goals, This Week I Will Focus On:

1. Spiritual: _____
2. Physical/Health: _____
3. Family/Relationship: _____
4. Financial: _____
5. Personal: _____

Sub-Tasks:

_____
_____
_____
_____

My Consistency Tracker:

_____ | Mon | Tue | Wed | Thu | Fri | Sat | Sun |

_____ | Mon | Tue | Wed | Thu | Fri | Sat | Sun |

My Water Consumption This Week (8x8oz Glasses Per-Day)

Monday	☐	☐	☐	☐	☐	☐	☐	☐
Tuesday	☐	☐	☐	☐	☐	☐	☐	☐
Wednesday	☐	☐	☐	☐	☐	☐	☐	☐
Thursday	☐	☐	☐	☐	☐	☐	☐	☐
Friday	☐	☐	☐	☐	☐	☐	☐	☐
Saturday	☐	☐	☐	☐	☐	☐	☐	☐
Sunday	☐	☐	☐	☐	☐	☐	☐	☐

Daily Focus

What's The Priority?!

Monday
1.
2.
3.

Tuesday
1.
2.
3.

Wednesday
1.
2.
3.

Thursday
1.
2.
3.

Friday
1.
2.
3.

Saturday
1.
2.
3.

Sunday
1.
2.
3.

Moment Of Gratitude

This Week I Am Thankful For:

Notes:

Monthly Recap

Reassess, Reset, Re-Focus

Reassess

This Month I Accomplished:

_____
_____
_____
_____
_____

I Allowed The Following Things To Distract Me:

_____
_____
_____
_____
_____

I Remained Consistent With:

_____
_____
_____
_____
_____

Monthly Recap

Reassess, Reset, Re-Focus

My Overall Assessment Of This Month:

_____
_____
_____
_____
_____
_____
_____

Reset
Next Month I Will Focus More On:

_____
_____
_____
_____
_____
_____
_____

Re-Focus
Review Your Yearly Goals And Your Why Statement To Keep You In-Focus Before Moving Into The Next Month.

Month: _____

My Goals This Month, In Alignment With My Yearly Goals Are:

1. Spiritual: _____
2. Physical/Health: _____
3. Family/Relationship: _____
4. Financial: _____
5. Personal: _____

I Will Accomplish These Goals By Doing The Following Things This Month:

_____
_____
_____
_____
_____
_____
_____
_____
_____
_____
_____

I Want To Remain Consistent With The Following Things This Month:

1. _____
2. _____

Tag Us On Instagram: @SheHasGoalsJournal

The Week Of:

In Alignment With My Monthly Goals, This Week I Will Focus On

3. Spiritual: _____
4. Physical/Health: _____
5. Family/Relationship: _____
6. Financial: _____
7. Personal: _____

Sub-Tasks:

_____
_____
_____
_____

My Consistency Tracker:

| _____ | Mon | Tue | Wed | Thu | Fri | Sat | Sun |
| _____ | Mon | Tue | Wed | Thu | Fri | Sat | Sun |

My Water Consumption This Week (8x8oz Glasses Per-Day)

Monday	☐ ☐ ☐ ☐ ☐ ☐ ☐ ☐
Tuesday	☐ ☐ ☐ ☐ ☐ ☐ ☐ ☐
Wednesday	☐ ☐ ☐ ☐ ☐ ☐ ☐ ☐
Thursday	☐ ☐ ☐ ☐ ☐ ☐ ☐ ☐
Friday	☐ ☐ ☐ ☐ ☐ ☐ ☐ ☐
Saturday	☐ ☐ ☐ ☐ ☐ ☐ ☐ ☐
Sunday	☐ ☐ ☐ ☐ ☐ ☐ ☐ ☐

Daily Focus

What's The Priority?!

Monday
1.
2.
3.

Tuesday
1.
2.
3.

Wednesday
1.
2.
3.

Thursday
1.
2.
3.

Friday
1.
2.
3.

Saturday
1.
2.
3.

Sunday
1.
2.
3.

Moment Of Gratitude

This Week I Am Thankful For:

Notes:

The Week Of:

In Alignment With My Monthly Goals, This Week I Will Focus On:

1. Spiritual: _____
2. Physical/Health: _____
3. Family/Relationship: _____
4. Financial: _____
5. Personal: _____

Sub-Tasks:

_____
_____
_____
_____

My Consistency Tracker:

_____	Mon	Tue	Wed	Thu	Fri	Sat	Sun
_____	Mon	Tue	Wed	Thu	Fri	Sat	Sun

My Water Consumption This Week (8x8oz Glasses Per-Day)

Monday	☐	☐	☐	☐	☐	☐	☐	☐
Tuesday	☐	☐	☐	☐	☐	☐	☐	☐
Wednesday	☐	☐	☐	☐	☐	☐	☐	☐
Thursday	☐	☐	☐	☐	☐	☐	☐	☐
Friday	☐	☐	☐	☐	☐	☐	☐	☐
Saturday	☐	☐	☐	☐	☐	☐	☐	☐
Sunday	☐	☐	☐	☐	☐	☐	☐	☐

Daily Focus

What's The Priority?!

Monday
1.
2.
3.

Tuesday
1.
2.
3.

Wednesday
1.
2.
3.

Thursday
1.
2.
3.

Friday
1.
2.
3.

Saturday
1.
2.
3.

Sunday
1.
2.
3.

Moment Of Gratitude

This Week I Am Thankful For:

Notes:

The Week Of:

In Alignment With My Monthly Goals, This Week I Will Focus On:

1. Spiritual: _____
2. Physical/Health: _____
3. Family/Relationship: _____
4. Financial: _____
5. Personal: _____

Sub-Tasks:

_____

_____

_____

_____

My Consistency Tracker:

	Mon	Tue	Wed	Thu	Fri	Sat	Sun
_____							
_____	Mon	Tue	Wed	Thu	Fri	Sat	Sun

My Water Consumption This Week (8x8oz Glasses Per-Day)

Monday ☐ ☐ ☐ ☐ ☐ ☐ ☐ ☐
Tuesday ☐ ☐ ☐ ☐ ☐ ☐ ☐ ☐
Wednesday ☐ ☐ ☐ ☐ ☐ ☐ ☐ ☐
Thursday ☐ ☐ ☐ ☐ ☐ ☐ ☐ ☐
Friday ☐ ☐ ☐ ☐ ☐ ☐ ☐ ☐
Saturday ☐ ☐ ☐ ☐ ☐ ☐ ☐ ☐
Sunday ☐ ☐ ☐ ☐ ☐ ☐ ☐ ☐

Daily Focus

What's The Priority?!

Monday
1.
2.
3.

Tuesday
1.
2.
3.

Wednesday
1.
2.
3.

Thursday
1.
2.
3.

Friday
1.
2.
3.

Saturday
1.
2.
3.

Sunday
1.
2.
3.

Moment Of Gratitude

This Week I Am Thankful For:

Notes:

The Week Of:

In Alignment With My Monthly Goals, This Week I Will Focus On:

1. Spiritual: _____
2. Physical/Health: _____
3. Family/Relationship: _____
4. Financial: _____
5. Personal: _____

Sub-Tasks:

_____

_____

_____

_____

My Consistency Tracker:

	Mon	Tue	Wed	Thu	Fri	Sat	Sun
_____							
_____	Mon	Tue	Wed	Thu	Fri	Sat	Sun

My Water Consumption This Week (8x8oz Glasses Per-Day)

Monday ☐ ☐ ☐ ☐ ☐ ☐ ☐ ☐

Tuesday ☐ ☐ ☐ ☐ ☐ ☐ ☐ ☐

Wednesday ☐ ☐ ☐ ☐ ☐ ☐ ☐ ☐

Thursday ☐ ☐ ☐ ☐ ☐ ☐ ☐ ☐

Friday ☐ ☐ ☐ ☐ ☐ ☐ ☐ ☐

Saturday ☐ ☐ ☐ ☐ ☐ ☐ ☐ ☐

Sunday ☐ ☐ ☐ ☐ ☐ ☐ ☐ ☐

Daily Focus

What's The Priority?!

Monday
1.
2.
3.

Tuesday
1.
2.
3.

Wednesday
1.
2.
3.

Thursday
1.
2.
3.

Friday
1.
2.
3.

Saturday
1.
2.
3.

Sunday
1.
2.
3.

Moment Of Gratitude

This Week I Am Thankful For:

Notes:

Monthly Recap

Reassess, Reset, Re-Focus

Reassess

This Month I Accomplished:

_____

_____

_____

_____

_____

I Allowed The Following Things To Distract Me:

_____

_____

_____

_____

_____

I Remained Consistent With:

_____

_____

_____

_____

_____

Monthly Recap

Reassess, Reset, Re-Focus

My Overall Assessment Of This Month:

_____
_____
_____
_____
_____
_____
_____

Reset
Next Month I Will Focus More On:

_____
_____
_____
_____
_____
_____
_____

Re-Focus
Review Your Yearly Goals And Your Why Statement To Keep You In-Focus Before Moving Into The Next Month.

Month: _____

My Goals This Month, In Alignment With My Yearly Goals Are:

1. Spiritual: _____
2. Physical/Health: _____
3. Family/Relationship: _____
4. Financial: _____
5. Personal: _____

I Will Accomplish These Goals By Doing The Following Things This Month:

_____
_____
_____
_____
_____
_____
_____
_____
_____
_____
_____

I Want To Remain Consistent With The Following Things This Month:

1. _____
2. _____

Tag Us On Instagram: @SheHasGoalsJournal

The Week Of:

In Alignment With My Monthly Goals, This Week I Will Focus On:

1. Spiritual:_____
2. Physical/Health: _____
3. Family/Relationship: _____
4. Financial: _____
5. Personal: _____

Sub-Tasks:

_____
_____
_____
_____

My Consistency Tracker:

	Mon	Tue	Wed	Thu	Fri	Sat	Sun
_____							
_____							

My Water Consumption This Week (8x8oz Glasses Per-Day)

Monday	☐	☐	☐	☐	☐	☐	☐	☐
Tuesday	☐	☐	☐	☐	☐	☐	☐	☐
Wednesday	☐	☐	☐	☐	☐	☐	☐	☐
Thursday	☐	☐	☐	☐	☐	☐	☐	☐
Friday	☐	☐	☐	☐	☐	☐	☐	☐
Saturday	☐	☐	☐	☐	☐	☐	☐	☐
Sunday	☐	☐	☐	☐	☐	☐	☐	☐

Daily Focus

What's The Priority?!

Monday
1.
2.
3.

Tuesday
1.
2.
3.

Wednesday
1.
2.
3.

Thursday
1.
2.
3.

Friday
1.
2.
3.

Saturday
1.
2.
3.

Sunday
1.
2.
3.

Moment Of Gratitude

This Week I Am Thankful For:

Notes:

The Week Of:

In Alignment With My Monthly Goals, This Week I Will Focus On:

1. Spiritual: _____
2. Physical/Health: _____
3. Family/Relationship: _____
4. Financial: _____
5. Personal: _____

Sub-Tasks:

_____
_____
_____
_____

My Consistency Tracker:

| _____ | Mon | Tue | Wed | Thu | Fri | Sat | Sun |
| _____ | Mon | Tue | Wed | Thu | Fri | Sat | Sun |

My Water Consumption This Week (8x8oz Glasses Per-Day)

Monday   ☐ ☐ ☐ ☐ ☐ ☐ ☐ ☐
Tuesday   ☐ ☐ ☐ ☐ ☐ ☐ ☐ ☐
Wednesday ☐ ☐ ☐ ☐ ☐ ☐ ☐ ☐
Thursday   ☐ ☐ ☐ ☐ ☐ ☐ ☐ ☐
Friday   ☐ ☐ ☐ ☐ ☐ ☐ ☐ ☐
Saturday   ☐ ☐ ☐ ☐ ☐ ☐ ☐ ☐
Sunday   ☐ ☐ ☐ ☐ ☐ ☐ ☐ ☐

Daily Focus

What's The Priority?!

Monday
1.
2.
3.

Tuesday
1.
2.
3.

Wednesday
1.
2.
3.

Thursday
1.
2.
3.

Friday
1.
2.
3.

Saturday
1.
2.
3.

Sunday
1.
2.
3.

Moment Of Gratitude

This Week I Am Thankful For:

Notes:

The Week Of:

In Alignment With My Monthly Goals, This Week I Will Focus On:

1. Spiritual: _____
2. Physical/Health: _____
3. Family/Relationship: _____
4. Financial: _____
5. Personal: _____

Sub-Tasks:

_____
_____
_____
_____

My Consistency Tracker:

| _____ | Mon | Tue | Wed | Thu | Fri | Sat | Sun |
| _____ | Mon | Tue | Wed | Thu | Fri | Sat | Sun |

My Water Consumption This Week (8x8oz Glasses Per-Day)

Monday	☐ ☐ ☐ ☐ ☐ ☐ ☐ ☐
Tuesday	☐ ☐ ☐ ☐ ☐ ☐ ☐ ☐
Wednesday	☐ ☐ ☐ ☐ ☐ ☐ ☐ ☐
Thursday	☐ ☐ ☐ ☐ ☐ ☐ ☐ ☐
Friday	☐ ☐ ☐ ☐ ☐ ☐ ☐ ☐
Saturday	☐ ☐ ☐ ☐ ☐ ☐ ☐ ☐
Sunday	☐ ☐ ☐ ☐ ☐ ☐ ☐ ☐

Daily Focus

What's The Priority?!

Monday
1.
2.
3.

Tuesday
1.
2.
3.

Wednesday
1.
2.
3.

Thursday
1.
2.
3.

Friday
1.
2.
3.

Saturday
1.
2.
3.

Sunday
1.
2.
3.

Moment Of Gratitude

This Week I Am Thankful For:

Notes:

The Week Of:

In Alignment With My Monthly Goals, This Week I Will Focus On:

1. Spiritual: _____
2. Physical/Health: _____
3. Family/Relationship: _____
4. Financial: _____
5. Personal: _____

Sub-Tasks:

_____
_____
_____
_____

My Consistency Tracker:

| _____ | Mon | Tue | Wed | Thu | Fri | Sat | Sun |
| _____ | Mon | Tue | Wed | Thu | Fri | Sat | Sun |

My Water Consumption This Week (8x8oz Glasses Per-Day)

Monday	☐	☐	☐	☐	☐	☐	☐	☐
Tuesday	☐	☐	☐	☐	☐	☐	☐	☐
Wednesday	☐	☐	☐	☐	☐	☐	☐	☐
Thursday	☐	☐	☐	☐	☐	☐	☐	☐
Friday	☐	☐	☐	☐	☐	☐	☐	☐
Saturday	☐	☐	☐	☐	☐	☐	☐	☐
Sunday	☐	☐	☐	☐	☐	☐	☐	☐

Daily Focus

What's The Priority?!

Monday
1.
2.
3.

Tuesday
1.
2.
3.

Wednesday
1.
2.
3.

Thursday
1.
2.
3.

Friday
1.
2.
3.

Saturday
1.
2.
3.

Sunday
1.
2.
3.

Moment Of Gratitude

This Week I Am Thankful For:

Notes:

Monthly Recap

Reassess, Reset, Re-Focus

Reassess
This Month I Accomplished:

_____
_____
_____
_____
_____

I Allowed The Following Things To Distract Me:

_____
_____
_____
_____
_____

I Remained Consistent With:

_____
_____
_____
_____
_____

Monthly Recap

Reassess, Reset, Re-Focus

My Overall Assessment Of This Month:

_____

_____

_____

_____

_____

_____

_____

Reset
Next Month I Will Focus More On:

_____

_____

_____

_____

_____

_____

_____

Re-Focus
Review Your Yearly Goals And Your Why Statement To Keep You In-Focus Before Moving Into The Next Month.

Month: _____

My Goals This Month, In Alignment With My Yearly Goals Are:

1. Spiritual: _____
2. Physical/Health: _____
3. Family/Relationship: _____
4. Financial: _____
5. Personal: _____

I Will Accomplish These Goals By Doing The Following Things This Month:

_____
_____
_____
_____
_____
_____
_____
_____
_____
_____
_____

I Want To Remain Consistent With The Following Things This Month:

1. _____
2. _____

Tag Us On Instagram: @SheHasGoalsJournal

The Week Of:

In Alignment With My Monthly Goals, This Week I Will Focus On

3. Spiritual: _____
4. Physical/Health: _____
5. Family/Relationship: _____
6. Financial: _____
7. Personal: _____

Sub-Tasks:

_____
_____
_____
_____

My Consistency Tracker:

	Mon	Tue	Wed	Thu	Fri	Sat	Sun
_____							
_____							

My Water Consumption This Week (8x8oz Glasses Per-Day)

Monday	☐	☐	☐	☐	☐	☐	☐	☐
Tuesday	☐	☐	☐	☐	☐	☐	☐	☐
Wednesday	☐	☐	☐	☐	☐	☐	☐	☐
Thursday	☐	☐	☐	☐	☐	☐	☐	☐
Friday	☐	☐	☐	☐	☐	☐	☐	☐
Saturday	☐	☐	☐	☐	☐	☐	☐	☐
Sunday	☐	☐	☐	☐	☐	☐	☐	☐

Daily Focus

What's The Priority?!

Monday
1.
2.
3.

Tuesday
1.
2.
3.

Wednesday
1.
2.
3.

Thursday
1.
2.
3.

Friday
1.
2.
3.

Saturday
1.
2.
3.

Sunday
1.
2.
3.

Moment Of Gratitude

This Week I Am Thankful For:

Notes:

The Week Of:

In Alignment With My Monthly Goals, This Week I Will Focus On:

1. Spiritual: _____
2. Physical/Health: _____
3. Family/Relationship: _____
4. Financial: _____
5. Personal: _____

Sub-Tasks:

_____
_____
_____
_____

My Consistency Tracker:

_____ | Mon | Tue | Wed | Thu | Fri | Sat | Sun |
_____ | Mon | Tue | Wed | Thu | Fri | Sat | Sun |

My Water Consumption This Week (8x8oz Glasses Per-Day)

Monday ☐ ☐ ☐ ☐ ☐ ☐ ☐ ☐
Tuesday ☐ ☐ ☐ ☐ ☐ ☐ ☐ ☐
Wednesday ☐ ☐ ☐ ☐ ☐ ☐ ☐ ☐
Thursday ☐ ☐ ☐ ☐ ☐ ☐ ☐ ☐
Friday ☐ ☐ ☐ ☐ ☐ ☐ ☐ ☐
Saturday ☐ ☐ ☐ ☐ ☐ ☐ ☐ ☐
Sunday ☐ ☐ ☐ ☐ ☐ ☐ ☐ ☐

Daily Focus

What's The Priority?!

Monday
1.
2.
3.

Tuesday
1.
2.
3.

Wednesday
1.
2.
3.

Thursday
1.
2.
3.

Friday
1.
2.
3.

Saturday
1.
2.
3.

Sunday
1.
2.
3.

Moment Of Gratitude

This Week I Am Thankful For:

Notes:

The Week Of:

In Alignment With My Monthly Goals, This Week I Will Focus On:

1. Spiritual: _____
2. Physical/Health: _____
3. Family/Relationship: _____
4. Financial: _____
5. Personal: _____

Sub-Tasks:

_____
_____
_____
_____

My Consistency Tracker:

| _____ | Mon | Tue | Wed | Thu | Fri | Sat | Sun |
| _____ | Mon | Tue | Wed | Thu | Fri | Sat | Sun |

My Water Consumption This Week (8x8oz Glasses Per-Day)

Monday	☐ ☐ ☐ ☐ ☐ ☐ ☐ ☐
Tuesday	☐ ☐ ☐ ☐ ☐ ☐ ☐ ☐
Wednesday	☐ ☐ ☐ ☐ ☐ ☐ ☐ ☐
Thursday	☐ ☐ ☐ ☐ ☐ ☐ ☐ ☐
Friday	☐ ☐ ☐ ☐ ☐ ☐ ☐ ☐
Saturday	☐ ☐ ☐ ☐ ☐ ☐ ☐ ☐
Sunday	☐ ☐ ☐ ☐ ☐ ☐ ☐ ☐

Daily Focus

What's The Priority?!

Monday
1.
2.
3.

Tuesday
1.
2.
3.

Wednesday
1.
2.
3.

Thursday
1.
2.
3.

Friday
1.
2.
3.

Saturday
1.
2.
3.

Sunday
1.
2.
3.

Moment Of Gratitude

This Week I Am Thankful For:

Notes:

The Week Of:

In Alignment With My Monthly Goals, This Week I Will Focus On:

1. Spiritual: _____
2. Physical/Health: _____
3. Family/Relationship: _____
4. Financial: _____
5. Personal: _____

Sub-Tasks:

_____
_____
_____
_____

My Consistency Tracker:

_____	Mon	Tue	Wed	Thu	Fri	Sat	Sun
_____	Mon	Tue	Wed	Thu	Fri	Sat	Sun

My Water Consumption This Week (8x8oz Glasses Per-Day)

Monday	☐ ☐ ☐ ☐ ☐ ☐ ☐ ☐
Tuesday	☐ ☐ ☐ ☐ ☐ ☐ ☐ ☐
Wednesday	☐ ☐ ☐ ☐ ☐ ☐ ☐ ☐
Thursday	☐ ☐ ☐ ☐ ☐ ☐ ☐ ☐
Friday	☐ ☐ ☐ ☐ ☐ ☐ ☐ ☐
Saturday	☐ ☐ ☐ ☐ ☐ ☐ ☐ ☐
Sunday	☐ ☐ ☐ ☐ ☐ ☐ ☐ ☐

Daily Focus

What's The Priority?!

Monday
1.
2.
3.

Tuesday
1.
2.
3.

Wednesday
1.
2.
3.

Thursday
1.
2.
3.

Friday
1.
2.
3.

Saturday
1.
2.
3.

Sunday
1.
2.
3.

Moment Of Gratitude

This Week I Am Thankful For:

Notes:

Monthly Recap

Reassess, Reset, Re-Focus

Reassess

This Month I Accomplished:

_____

_____

_____

_____

_____

I Allowed The Following Things To Distract Me:

_____

_____

_____

_____

_____

I Remained Consistent With:

_____

_____

_____

_____

_____

Monthly Recap

Reassess, Reset, Re-Focus

My Overall Assessment Of This Month:

_____
_____
_____
_____
_____
_____
_____

Reset
Next Month I Will Focus More On:

_____
_____
_____
_____
_____
_____
_____

Re-Focus
Review Your Yearly Goals And Your Why Statement To Keep You In-Focus Before Moving Into The Next Month.

A Year In Review

This Year I Accomplished:

243

A Year In Review

My Overall Assessment Of This Year:

End Of The Year Remarks

Wow, congratulations you made it! Take a look at how far you've come and how much you've grown over the past few months. Doesn't it feel great to be able to track your progress?

As you look back over your year I'm sure it wasn't easy. There may have been many hurdles to jump but the most important thing is you didn't allow those hurdles to stifle you.

Celebrate your wins, learn from your losses and grow from your mistakes. Whatever you do, just keep going.

You now have a journal documenting your 2022 journey. Keep it and use it to compare your progress in 2023.

Order your 2023 She Has Goals® journal today!
www.shehasgoalsjournal.com

With Love,
Nikela (Nikki) Kelley
"Your Accountability Coach"

© 2021 Kelley's Prints